GLASS PAPERWEIGHTS
AN OLD CRAFT REVIVED

Glass Paperweights

an old craft revived

by

Paul Hollister

William Culross & Son Limited
Coupar Angus, Scotland

ISBN 0 900323 18 3

Printed in Scotland by
William Culross & Son Limited, Coupar Angus, Perthshire

CONTENTS

LIST OF ILLUSTRATIONS

PREFACE

In 1967 an American friend gave Stuart Drysdale, manager of a small Scottish glass factory, an outdated copy of the American magazine *Woman's Day*; the issue had appeared in July, 1965. The cover illustration showed a variety of glass paperweights, and inside there was an article on the famous Bergstrom paperweight collection in Neenah, Wisconsin, long considered the mecca for antique glass paperweights. About a hundred paperweights of many varieties from the collection were illustrated in color, and, when Drysdale studied them, and showed the magazine to some of his glass-blowers, a vista opened that was to change their lives.

Glass paperweights were first made in continental Europe in the 1840s, and the best known producers were the French factories of Baccarat, St. Louis, and Clichy. These French paperweights have been so widely written about and acclaimed that today they are avidly sought by collectors, who find them increasingly expensive and in dwindling supply. But to Stuart Drysdale in 1967 the word Baccarat stood for a card game, while St. Louis was a town somewhere on the Mississippi.

The late nineteenth and early twentieth centuries saw sporadic attempts in Europe and America to duplicate or improve upon French paper-weights of the 1840s, but it took a century for the historical impulse to return. After World War II a genuine revival began that was spontaneous and, eventually, worldwide. The range of countries where glass paper-weights are made today extends from Scandinavia to China. Though there are several one-man, and numerous two-man and four-man paperweight making operations in various countries, Stuart Drysdale's factory, Perth-shire Paperweights Limited, stands practically alone as the only factory-sized operation (Perthshire employs twenty-five men and women) devoted exclusively to making these lovely and much sought after objects.

In August of 1974 I spent a week at the Perthshire Paperweights factory, free to observe every phase of paperweight making, to watch each step repeated as many times as I needed in order to understand it, and to ask any questions that came to mind. With a few minor exceptions I was encouraged to reveal technical procedures that, in paperweight making circles, might be considered trade secrets. One exception involved a logical solution to a persistent problem that was solved by men at Perthshire, as it must have been solved repeatedly by other paperweight makers over the past one hundred and thirty years. Another concerned the revival of a technique that was certainly no secret in ancient times and has been reapplied in recent years—in my view with limited success. Stuart Drysdale believes that 'Other glass factories are not likely to copy us. If they want to, alright: we need good competition to protect our future and our continuity.'

This is a progress report on a twentieth century attempt to revive a nineteenth century craft. Here also, for the first time, is a step-by-step explanation of how many different types of paperweights are actually made.

CHAPTER I

In 1960 Stuart Drysdale, a country lawyer in Crieff, Scotland, was persuaded to take over the management of Vasart Glass Limited, a small factory making glass paperweights and vases in a collection of ramshackle wooden sheds by the River Tay in Perth, the county seat of Perthshire. The paperweights were all marketed in London, and in those days the factory price was two shillings and sixpence for the miniature size, four shillings for the medium, and six shillings and sixpence for the large size, which was about three inches in diameter. Some miniatures were sold to a firm called Lassman that made bar fittings, and appeared on the handle end of corkscrews, bottle openers and the like.

Through a peculiar combination of circumstances Vasart also made squashed bottles for Teachers Whisky, and undertook to fill an order for light globes to be used in the reconstruction of No. 10 Downing Street. The squashed bottles were ashtrays made from melted whisky bottles, an idea conceived by a prankster at a party who put a whisky bottle in a pottery kiln, and found when he removed it that it was flattened out and curved up at the ends. Though not very challenging to Drysdale's imagination, squashed bottles were easy enough to make. But the enormous light globes called for in the Downing Street architect's plans taxed Vasart ingenuity and facilities to the limit. Twenty were ordered, but each one required an eleven-man team and filled a kiln. All other production had to be halted, yet for months they were unable to produce a single globe. Finally, the twenty globes were produced and Vasart was paid about one hundred and fifty pounds apiece for them, which, though fair enough of itself, was about a third what they had cost to make.

After losing money for two years, at the end of 1963 Vasart broke even, and Drysdale hoped to raise money for an efficient modern factory. The money came from Teachers Whisky, who became at the same time majority stockholder and owner. At the end of 1964 the dilapidated sheds of Vasart Glass Limited were bulldozed into the Tay and a new factory, which Drysdale helped to design, was built in his home town of Crieff, eighteen miles west of Perth. It was called Strathearn Glass and Drysdale was its manager. In 1966 Strathearn showed a profit for the first time.

But in February, 1968, Stuart Drysdale left Strathearn Glass and, with urging and encouragement from several of his former glassworkers, decided to start his own company devoted exclusively to making paperweights. He called the venture Perthshire Paperweights Limited. 'In Britain,' says Drysdale, 'many people have been running away from the computerized, mass production life, trying to get back into the old-fashioned crafts. There's a great deal of promotion to encourage these worthy ventures, but they are seldom commercially viable. And this is my hobbyhorse: I think the first essential is to have a sound commercial basis for these worthy crafts.'

Commencing frugally, Drysdale settled for his craft venture on an abandoned school in Crieff that was to serve as his paperweight factory for the next two years. A building permit was obtained, materials ordered, and a furnace builder rounded up. John Deacons, a strapping lad of sixteen who had worked for Drysdale at Strathearn, came over to help with the strenuous building of the furnace. At the end of June, 1968, Drysdale and Deacons were joined by Jack Allen, who had been at Vasart, and by two teenage apprentices from Strathearn, Roy MacDonald and Peter Macdougall, boys who had done little more than carry paperweights to the annealing kiln. The occasion was the lighting of the furnace tank.

It takes about two months to bring a new tank furnace into operation without cracking it. The tank has to be warmed up slowly with a small gas-jet ring, raising the temperature about 150 degrees over two weeks. After four weeks the big burners are turned on, but it takes altogether about seven weeks to bring the tank to the stage where glass can be blown. Even then the first batch or melt picks up cement and other detritus from the building of the furnace, and three or four melts are required before the glass is clear enough to use. In July, while Drysdale made a trip to Germany to obtain color supplies, Anton 'Tony' Moravec came over from Strathearn to act as factory manager. The whole venture was launched on fifteen hundred pounds, and in August, 1968, the first Perthshire paperweight was made.

Like most new businesses trying to get started the firm that first year lost money. Added to the usual difficulties was the challenge of an unexpected order placed by the London paperweight dealer, Alan Tillman, for the first quality weight Drysdale had ever attempted to make, a red, white and blue crown paperweight. 'While the design of a crown weight may seem simple enough, with all the twisted ribbons meeting at the top,' Drysdale says, 'one has to remember that the corkscrew twists of the various ribbon canes are only approximately equal. And the colors we used, the red and the blue varied from dark to pale, even in the same cane. The setup girl had to select from an enormous tray of twisted canes to get ten near enough alike in color and spiral to go into each weight.' The crown paperweight, time-consuming and therefore expensive to make, was not an unqualified success. Drysdale brooded that if they were really stuck he could always fall back on making glass bullions (bulls-eyes) and selling them at a nice profit to pubs, inns, and other creators of antique atmosphere. 'But we never made them; and after the crown paperweight our next "special" weights were all sold out in a few weeks. Since then we've grown and grown.'

Perthshire made glass in the old school from August of '68 to October of 1970, when they simply outgrew the space and Drysdale had to look for a new location.

Crieff is built on a hillside, and the flat, open land at the lower end of town belongs to the Drummond Castle Estate. The land Drysdale acquired from the Estate on the road to Muthill must at one time have been used as a dumping ground for stones and rubble, because the subsoil is loosely compacted and unstable. To compensate for this Drysdale asked for the two furnaces he planned to be isolated on two concrete platforms, each twelve to eighteen inches thick, so that if one foundation cracked the cracks would not spread, as they tend to do, across the whole floor of the factory.

The first furnace built did not crack, it sank three inches, breaking the foundation blocks and causing endless trouble with stones and cords in the glass. When they dug up the platform they discovered the contractor had cheated and the platform was only six inches thick. So, taking what he thought was no chances, Drysdale had four feet of concrete poured beneath the place where the second tank was to be built. The second tank did not sink but it never worked well either, for reasons that were never completely clear—it may have been brought up to melting temperature too rapidly.

Stuart Drysdale has lived with furnace troubles since the Vasart days and knows the things that can go wrong. A tank furnace's function is, of course, to melt glass; and in the melting process there is a close interaction between the receptacle and its contents. The walls of the furnace are made from blocks of silica, which is itself the primary ingredient of glass. As the walls age and cracks form, the melting glass attacks the blocks and little chips of silica break off and fuse slowly into the glass, causing cords (striations). Drysdale used to buy sillimanite blocks from English furnace builders, but with his new furnaces he has switched to Zak, a very expensive silica block imported from the south of France that is more resistant to attack by the contents of the furnace.

The first of the new tanks was built in the spring of 1973. To make absolutely sure this time that the furnace foundations would not sink or crack, a trench twelve feet deep was dug for each furnace and filled with concrete. The first tank was lit during the summer and performed so well that the old tank, the one that had never really worked well, was shut down. A second tank was completed in November of '73 and lit in the spring of '74, at the time during the power shortage when the three-day week was lifted.

The blocks for a third tank await assembly on another concrete platform. Drysdale says, 'It was all horribly expensive, but good glass is essential no matter what it costs.'

The new factory was financed on seven thousand pounds. This money was raised by Drysdale and some of the glassworkers who had shares in the business. The whole thing was paid for with no overdraft and no borrowing.

CHAPTER II

The Perthshire paperweight factory down on the Muthill Road is a rather plain, rectangular building perhaps one hundred feet long by fifty feet wide, with blue siding and white trim around the doors, and a low hip roof perforated by one small ventilator. The building stands just off the road behind a prim white fence, and is reached by a short drive ending in a small car park bordered by the factory dump, an open bin about ten by six feet, walled on three sides with cinderblock. A sign at the fence is intended to discourage interruptions by casual visitors; people who have written ahead asking to see the works have generally been accommodated. The chief reason for the sign is that, unlike many glass factories, Perthshire has no area way provided for visitors. It has no showroom for examples of its paperweights and no salesroom for 'factory seconds,' that is paperweights not considered up to standard. Those weights are thrown in the dump in a procedure to be described later. It is not possible to buy a Perthshire paperweight at the factory.

The interior of the factory is as austere as the exterior. A large blowing room, the heart of any glass factory, occupies most of the space. In what little space is left there are two small stock rooms, one for coloring agents and bars of colored glass, the other for heavier glass ingredients such as sand and red lead (litharge). There's a room where the weights are stored on shelves as they come from the annealing kilns, and where they are checked for flaws and packed for shipment. There's a grinding room, and another small room used by some of the girls who arrange the designs for the common or 'bread and butter' weights, as Drysdale calls them. A small projection at a rear corner of the factory contains a canteen and a room shared by a lampworker and the girls who set up the more expensive weights. And that's it. I noticed that there was not even an office for Stuart Drysdale or for his factory manager, Tony Moravec. When I asked Drysdale about this he replied, as he so often does, with a cautionary story, a parable if you like.

'A man came to see me once from a far bigger factory than ours that was having problems, and he said to me, "Is there somewhere we can talk?" I took him into my warehouse and I said, "We can talk here." And he said,

"Where is your office?" I said, "We've got no office." He seemed surprised but shrugged it off. "Why I want to speak to you," he said, "is because I wonder why you're succeeding so soon and we're not?" And I said, "Well, the answer is right before you: there is no office. I've always wanted to get the nitty-gritty right first, and we can afford the things that go round it later on—the comfortable chairs and the canned music."' The canteen and the room for the lampworker are *luxuries* only recently added.

For anyone not familiar with the sights, sounds, temperatures, and procedures of glassworking, paperweight making at Perthshire is a remarkable experience, like a visit to an alchemist's.

Only a few feet from the hot roar of the blowing room, in the compacted silence of the stock-and-packing room, Janette Robertson arranges the contents of the scrambled paperweights in a flat iron ring mold with a pair of tweezers. (Two interesting points right here: I was puzzled as to why the design inside a paperweight, which appears somewhat dome-shaped when viewed in profile, should be arranged in a flat mold. The answer to that is that the domed shape is later imparted naturally, automatically in the procedure that shapes the outer gathers of glass. The other point is that brass molds are used for the better paperweights because they pick up less dust. Some dust is burned off when the cane design is heated in the next step.) But to get back to Miss Robertson; like the beak of a bird her tweezers sift and strike through cardboard boxes filled with random colored chips and slices of cane that are scrap from the cane making process, rejecting this fragment, selecting that with a fussiness that seems to contradict the casual appearance we associate with the scrambled or pell-mell design.

Miss Robertson has been with Perthshire from the beginning and obviously knows what she's doing; so I ask her about this. She replies, 'We try to fill in all the gaps and leave no air holes. When the boys make the scrambled weights they roll the hot glass over the finer powdered scraps to make a background before they pick up my design; and that fills in the gaps.' There are no gaps-of-light spaces in Miss Robertson's scrambleds, which is something antique American paperweight makers, at least, didn't bother much about. Miss Robertson's tweezers move deftly, finding a concave chip from a large cane that will cradle a smaller convex slice. She does this in isolation by the hour.

But Janette Robertson also screens all the Perthshire weights for defects. She can spot a tiny bubble, a stone or cord in the glass, a leaf tip on a flower that is not quite right, or any of a dozen others defects the casual viewer might not notice. The weights are all inspected twice, once when they're taken from the annealing kiln and put on shelves in the stockroom, and once again before packing. Referring to Miss Robertson, factory manager

Tony Moravec says, 'Hawk-eyes comes to me and says, "Look at that! There's a white spot on the edge of the 'P' (for Perthshire) cane." She won't pass it if the defect spoils the design of one of the more expensive weights. With the cheaper weights she is less strict.'

When she sees a defective paperweight, Janette Robertson picks up another defective weight and knocks them together several times, each impact making a brutal, billiard carom click that leaves a large moon bruise on each weight. After doing this several times she casually chucks them into a cardboard carton. Thus no badly flawed weight leaves the factory or can be sold as a 'factory second.' By Friday one or two cartons are filled with rejects. Out the stockroom window is a glimpse of the dump and, beyond it, a small contractor's yard with a truck tossed upside down. Drysdale swears there is a fine view of the Grampian Mountains out that window, but it was lost in fog and rain the week I was there.

Designs for what Stuart Drysdale calls the 'bread and butter' weights are made up by five or six girls in the cane room. These weights are generally concentrics, that is designs composed of concentric circles of canes, and they come in two sizes: medium, with a diameter of two-and-a-half inches, and large, with a diameter of three inches. Yet the designs themselves, the actual arrangements the girls make of the canes, fit into cast iron molds of, respectively, one and three-sixteenth and two and three-sixteenth inches diameter. Nevertheless, when covered with glass the designs appear to fill completely the glass of the paperweight domes. The difference between the reality and the illusion is due to the magnifying properties of convexly curved glass, and accounts in large part for the crystal ball mysteriousness of paperweights and the uncanny attraction they have for us. For many of the concentrics a wheel-spoked arrangement of thin, filigree (twisted) rods compartmentalizes the canes and keeps the design neat and even. This convenient spoke design was first used by the now famous contemporary paperweight maker Paul Ysart and his brothers in the old Moncrieff and Vasart days. But at Perthshire it is only used now for the standard weights.

When a dozen designs are completed in their molds they are carried to the blowing room like so many unleavened cakes on a tray, to be made into paperweights.

To anyone who has never seen a millefiori paperweight made, the process by which a pumpkin of a design is transformed into a golden coach is shrouded in mystery and misconception. In actual fact the process appears deceptively simple.

In the blowing room one of several craftsmen making the concentrics selects a mold with its completed cane design and places it to heat up just below the mouth of the glory hole, that small, empty furnace where glass is reheated while being worked. If the design were not preheated it might crack during the making. To heat it further he transfers the mold design to a grill above a gas burner flame, enclosing the design with an iron cylinder and covering the top with a small metal sheet. Critical to the paperweight making process is the craftsman's ability to gauge the temperature of both the heated canes and the ball of glass with which they are gradually covered. Too great a discrepancy in temperature between the two can result in a slushy design or a paperweight full of bubbles.

Meanwhile, the craftsman has gone to the furnace tank and gathered on the end of his pontil rod a small, glowing, orange gob of clear glass, which he marvers (shapes) to cylinder shape on an iron marver (table) in front of the glory hole, until it is compactly formed and free of bubbles. He then rolls this shaped gather in a curved pan filled with powdered, coloured glass that serves as background color for his design, reheating it at the glory hole to make the colored flakes blend to a solid tone, reshaping it on the marver until it is the shape and size to fill the mold. Then, with pontil rod held vertically and high above the design, he lets the glass-tipped rod descend briefly but decisively into the cylinder mold, where the preheated design now adheres to the cylindrical glass gob with its colored ground. Immediately he withdraws the pontil with its now imprisoned design. Imagine lowering an iron rod weighing six or eight pounds slowly and accurately into a mold two inches in diameter and you have the problem—it looks a good deal easier than it is.

The exposed design now has to be covered with the clear glass that will make it a paperweight, and this requires several trips to the furnace to gather more glass and, between each trip, the shaping of the growing ball of glass. One of the commonest and most characteristic sights of any glass-house is that of the craftsman or gaffer constantly rolling the blowing iron or pontil rod forwards and backwards on the arms of his chair to keep the still-soft glass from sagging off the rod or losing its shape. Rotation actually makes it easier to achieve the uniform roundness of any object, whether turned wood, clay on the wheel, or a glass vessel or paperweight on a rod. Rotation also helps the craftsman to cut in behind the design with that ancient tool, the pucellas, and to shape and smooth the crown of the paper-weight with a time-honored wooden block, or with the equally effective pad. These homemade pads, which may be nothing more than a wad of com-pacted, wetted newspaper or tissue paper, are individually concocted and as personal to the user as a baseball mitt is to the catcher.

Finally, when the attractively domed curve of the weight is achieved, the craftsman checks the diameter with calipers—diameters for each size

Top left—Arranging scrambled weight canes
Top right—Designing concentrics
Below—Gathering design from mould

paperweight must be consistent—and strikes the pontil a few inches behind the weight with a file or any handy metal tool, knocking the weight off the rod into a metal box filled with fine sand. The sand comes from Loch Aline up on the West Coast of Scotland and is the same sand as is used to make the Perthshire glass. The paperweight, the gathers of which left the furnace at the normal working temperature of about 1200 degrees centigrade (2192 degrees Fahrenheit) has by now cooled to about 500 degrees centigrade, so the sand doesn't scratch it. Now, while the glass is still slightly plastic, the mark left by separation of the weight from the pontil is depressed with a steel die to concave it. (The more expensive weights have the base hollow ground to remove all trace of the pontil.) The craftsman or his servitor now carries the completed weight on a perforated shovel—which lets the sand fall away—to the annealing kiln, where it cools at a gradual, controlled rate for twenty-four hours, before removal from the kiln, inspection, and consequent storage or rejection. The whole operation in the blowing room has taken about seven minutes.

Without artificial lighting, the big blowing room has a special tawny gloom given it by the hot white glow of the furnaces, the burnt orange blooms of hot glass swung about on rods, and by faint patches of northern daylight. The netherworld scene simmers with the roaring breath of the glass furnaces, the heat mitigated only slightly by big floor fans. (To be there alone at night, with the fans shut off, the building closed, and the heat even fiercer, is almost frightening, like standing near a live volcano. For, of course, the furnaces are never shut down.) In this hot din the glassworkers perform age-old tasks, moving in rhythms that have not changed in centuries. Of necessity glassmaking is largely pantomime; communication is by example and with the eyes, though occasionally members of a glass team will shout inexpletives at one another, which are carried out of hearing by the cooling fans.

All twelve who work in the blowing room, from the greenest apprentice to the most skilled craftsman, are required part of the time to make the simpler weights. While a few are content to continue doing this, many go on to learn more ambitious tasks and tricks, for there is an undercurrent of competition and rivalry that is contagious in the hot atmosphere of the blowing room.

Apprentices usually begin at the school-leaving age of fifteen or sixteen. Some learn the glass ways in as little as two years, but most take five. To learn by imitation is the natural and often the only way, and the team system used for making the more complicated paperweights affords repeated opportunities for imitation. Also, the more experienced workers are required to teach those less skilled. The level of skill is tested when a paperweight is checked for flaws; but the skills are developed in teamwork where timing, such as the more complicated weights require, is decisive. Here a team of two or three synchronize their actions in a ballet of timed gesture that produces a paperweight in a matter of minutes.

When he makes a paperweight with a two-color overlay, for instance, John Deacons requires a servitor (assistant). To make the overlay itself Deacons has to 'blow a cup.' As always with glassblowing, the process begins with a gob of clear glass gathered on the end of the blowpipe. Alternately marvered, blown, and shaped in a wetted fruitwood block, the foggy-orange bubble has grown to the size of a small light bulb. Enter now the servitor with a rod tipped with a gather of opaque white (which also glows orange). Working in tandem the two join the opaque gather to the top of the bubble; then Deacons scissors it off the rod, pulling it down like reluctant molasses over the clear bubble, now heating it at the glory hole to flow the overlay smoothly over the bubble, which it has to cover with a uniform thickness. Followed by more shaping. The servitor, in the meantime, has gathered opaque green (again, it glows orange) on another rod, and the two now repeat the covering process, this time dragging the green down over the opaque white. Deacons blows the three-layered bubble larger, reheating it, shaping it again. For a third time and with a third iron the servitor returns. This iron is topped with a button of clear glass, and they attach it to the top of the bubble so the top can be more easily cracked off—which they now proceed carefully to do. Then Deacons heats the resulting jagged cup at the glory hole, turning and turning it till it resembles a lovely Venetian goblet. In all this the orange glow of clear and colored glass alike has made it difficult to tell if the overlay colors are even in cohesion, tone, and thickness.

But the blown cup is only the first stage in the overlay process. If the overlay cup is intended as decoration for the surface of the weight, as for an overlay paperweight, then the servitor has to mark time with the completed cup, maintaining its shape and temperature, while Deacons makes the actual clear glass paperweight with its colored design. When that is completed the two come together, and Deacons slowly lowers the big, clear ball of the paperweight he has just made, letting the heavy iron settle the orange ball into the cup, which it fills like a devil's elixir. It takes a keen eye to make a paperweight of exactly the size to fit the overlay cup—if the ball is too small the design will be lost inside the cup and will probably not be centred. Finally, Deacons goes once more to the furnace for a thin coating of clear glass to cover the overlay, checking with the pucellas to remove any bubbles before he cuts in the base and cracks off the weight.

Another use for the overlay cup is as a color ground beneath the design. Here the blown cup is filled not with the paperweight ball but with a gather of clear glass, then sealed up, and used to pick up the paperweight design from its mold. The design on its overlaid, shaped cushion is then covered with clear glass until the desired paperweight size is reached. If the interior design chosen would not completely cover the gap left at the clipped end of the cup where the layers of exposed overlay would distract from the design, the filled overlay cup can be transferred to another rod attached at right angles to the first rod, so that an area of unblemished overlay is behind the design.

Big John Deacons is not always successful with his overlays. Recently, as an experiment, he tried to encase a double overlay paperweight with a thick layer of clear glass in the manner of the St. Louis factory in nineteenth century France. The few encased overlays St. Louis made are today out of reach of all but the wealthiest collectors. George Bacchus & Sons, of England, were the only other factory known to have attempted encased overlays, and their efforts were rarely successful. To Deacons, who is only twenty-three, this was a challenge.

Manager Tony Moravec showed me the result. Deacons had been able to encase the green over opaque white double overlay, with its cut windows in clear glass. While this was a triumph in itself—because the weight had had to be reheated very slowly (after the windows were cut) to a temperature where it could amalgamate with new, hot glass—Deacons had heated it up so much and covered it so slowly that the outer layer of clear glass had dragged the green overlay askew over the white, so that Moravec's precision-cut windows now looked wobbly. As Moravec put it, without rancor, 'I spent two hours facetting that weight, and he goes into the tank and within two minutes he spoils it.'

Like most new paperweights the men at Perthshire try, this encased overlay will be attempted dozens of times before the result warrants production. Once in production, the percentage of rejects will probably run high. 'We have no set pattern,' says Moravec, 'We're learning all the time. When we start doing a thing and it doesn't work out, we've got to find the fault and start fresh again. Sometimes it's rather frustrating!'

Many of the frustrations occurred when they were just getting started at Perthshire. Stuart Drysdale laughs about it now, but his is the jocularity of retrospect. 'We bought some cameos from a cameo factory and tried putting one—as if it were a sulphide—into a paperweight. It just got smaller, and smaller, and smaller, and it completely vanished. We had a similar experience trying to make a swan silhouette cane; we made the shape alright, but every time we pulled out the cane the thin neck vanished.'

However, Drysdale never saw Perthshire as making reproductions of nineteenth century paperweights. 'We would look at the old weights and try to figure out how they did it, and then do it ourselves with our own designs.' In other words, they are trying to put old techniques to the service of new ideas and designs, a challenge that is particularly difficult with glass,

Top left—Uncovered concentric weight
Top right—Gathering from furnace
Below—Filling overlay cup

because technical procedures, nominally a part of glassworking tradition, are in many instances carefully guarded secrets that are not passed on, each new generation of glassmakers having to learn largely from scratch.

What they see in the old weights is not always edifying. Tony Moravec says, 'They shock us, some of them; they're dirty, they're cordy, the flowers are dusty, and there's marks on them.' I asked him about the faint outline one sometimes sees above the design in old weights. 'That comes if the glass inside is too cold when they make the new gathers, and it leaves a faint outline between layers. Or it could be from padding (shaping) with a dirty pad. It leaves tiny bubbles he can't hardly see, and when he goes and covers it the bubbles are caught.'

The shock Moravec feels at the imperfections of some old weights may come as a shock to collectors of these treasures as well; but it is almost certain that at Perthshire more people are putting more time and effort toward the solution of technical paperweight problems and toward the production of defect-free weights than was the case with any of the big, speciality glass factories of the nineteenth century where paperweights—with the possible exception of the Clichy factory—were generally a sideline.

It should be obvious by now that the paperweights made at Perthshire are not the result of solo operations but the combined efforts of several people. We began by watching Janette Robertson arrange cane scraps in a die (mold) for a scrambled weight. Let's go back a step further and consider the basic ingredient of all millefiori paperweights, the canes themselves. How are they made?

Cane making is not only basic, it is historically the earliest glassmaking procedure adopted by makers of paperweights, dating from the beginning of the Christian era in Alexandria and Rome. A cane is composed of one or more rods of colored glass assembled and processed to show a continuous design. The term *millefiori* (Italian for thousand flowers) is now thought to have been coined in the nineteenth century in Germany, and describes the effect of many juxtaposed canes seen in cross-section slices. Depending on the design required and the techniques used, cane making can be a simple or a complicated process.

The relatively simple bullseye cane can be made freehand, that is without using a mold. This cane, which resembles a target, is composed of concentric rings of color separated by clear glass. To begin a four-ring bullseye the craftsman marvers a gather of opaque white glass until it is evenly cylindrical. He then rolls the glass cylinder in a metal trough filled with powdered and fragmented red glass, say, which a second man has already heated with a blowtorch. He marvers the two-colored cylinder, reheats it at the glory hole, covers it with a layer of clear glass from the furnace, marvers again, rolls it once more in the trough of red; repeating the whole process four times. By now the bullseye cane is perhaps two inches in diameter and six inches long.

After reheating once again at the glory hole, the other end of the bullseye cane is attached to a second pontil, and the two men—facing one another with their pontils held horizontal under a good deal of tension, and rotated slowly to keep the circular cane from sagging to oval shape—pull (back) slowly away from one another, until the cane is stretched to a length of perhaps five feet and is now only pencil thick. The cane by now is cool enough not to pick up dirt and can be lowered carefully to the floor. The men, first one, then the other, crack the cane from their pontils, and one, using the stump end of the cane still attached to his pontil, breaks the cane with it into foot-long segments. In spite of the care taken, only two feet of cane is found to be perfectly round and usable, and these lengths are placed in the kiln to anneal properly. Otherwise, even though thin, they would eventually crack or shatter.

Thus, three men were involved in the operation for ten or fifteen minutes, and all they got was two usable feet of cane. And this is only one cane out of dozens of cane patterns that may be used in a single design. At the very best ten good lengths of three to four inches each are salvageable from some of these canes. For this expensive reason the distorted oval segments of cane are not thrown out, but are sliced up for use in the casual scrambled weights already described.

Other varieties of cane, with cogged or scalloped edges, are colored in the overlay manner with a gob of one color topping and pulled down over another, and the cane shapes are imparted by a series of preheated iron molds about the size and shape of an old-fashioned glass (whisky tumbler). The craftsman lowers the cane-tipped pontil into the mold, forcing the glass evenly and firmly against the interior mold design, which is sloped slightly inward to ease removal of the impressed glass. Thus the growing cane has to be marvered back to cylinder shape between each new molding. The completed cane is then pulled out as all canes are, and cut into manageable lengths.

A large, complex cane, perhaps intended for the center piece of a paperweight design, may be assembled from as many as six or eight canes such as those just described. Selections are made from large bundles of identically designed and colored canes, the supply bundles contained with rubber bands. Each new, multiple cane (florette) measures approximately five inches long by two inches in diameter.

Once the components of the large cane have been assembled and tied with copper wire, the cane must be heated until the components coalesce and it can be covered with the protective layer of clear glass used to seal all glass elements that go into paperweights. Formerly the cane was held together during heating by a copper wire tied about the middle of the cane bundle, until it was discovered that when the bundle was heated, the copper wire left a black mark that seemed to eat into the glass, and stretched to foot-long black smudges when the cane was pulled out. The simple remedy proved to be to wind the easy-to-tie copper wire about each end of the bundle, where the black mark would be cut off automatically in the cane making process after the cane was pulled.

Perhaps most interesting to watch is the making of the twist or filigree canes that form the spoke arrangement of the common weights, but are also used for the lace grounds and even for the wings of dragonflies. Twisted canes were made in ancient Rome to decorate the rims of millefiori bowls. But they are more generally known from their extensive use in Venetian sixteenth century latticinio vessels and in the stems of eighteenth century English drinking glasses. Glass literature abounds in illustrated descriptions of a mold fluted on the inside where it is lined vertically with opaque white rods alternating with clear glass rods, with perhaps every third or fourth rod a color rod. The pontil with its shaped gather is lowered into the mold and, upon withdrawal, is attached to a second rod; only this time, instead of merely being pulled out thin, the cane is also twisted in opposite directions by the men on the ends.

At Perthshire the procedure is enlivened by a hand-cranked twisting device to which one hot end of the cane is attached, the operator at that end being able to regulate the speed with which the cane is twisted, and therefore also the tightness or looseness of the spiral, while the fellow on the other end rotates the cane in the usual way. It is fascinating to watch the lengthening, hot glass cane making skiprope arcs in the air as the man at the free end backs off now ten feet, now fifteen, now twenty or more, and the rapidly cooling and diminishing glass remains elastic and in one piece, with the twist design delicately reduced to a miniature of the original. I watched Peter MacDougall and Stevenson Mackay work the filigree rods in tandem a dozen times. Mackay is seventeen years old and about five feet tall and he whistles while he works, like the seasoned professional he is. He says he wants to go to America, and Stuart Drysdale, in a rare moment of panic, assures him they won't let him into the country, he's too short.

When he isn't pulling filigree rods Stevenson Mackay snips them into one-inch lengths with a pair of pliers, letting the lengths fall into a large cardboard box labelled CARLSBERG THE GLORIOUS BEER OF COPENHAGEN, as supply for lace grounds which show off the colored canes to such advantage. It looked so easy I asked Mackay if I could try, and he handed me cane and pliers. The filigree rod is no thicker than three-sixteenths of an inch and the pliers were sharp, but I couldn't break the rod. It requires a sharp twist of the wrist to snap off a segment, and when I finally got the knack, the severed ends were jagged. Mackay tried not to smile.

Top—Stretching and twisting canes
Below left—Assembling flower by lampwork
Below right—Shaping dome of weight

To make a lace ground the snips of filigree are dumped into an iron cylinder and heated with a torch until stuck together like so much hot rice, then picked up on the pontil gather and marvered, and, finally, lowered onto the metal disc with its cane design, the paperweight being finished in the usual way.

All of the paperweight designs not composed of cane elements, such as flowers and insects, are made by the process called lampwork. Angus Hutchison, who had been working for John Moncrieff glassworks in Perth, making intricate forms of scientific laboratory glass with a blow lamp, joined Perthshire in late 1969. He had never done paperweight lampwork before. Today his skill is remarkable. Seated at the end of a long white table used by the girls who arrange the paperweight designs, he waves his torch like an oriental magician, and bits of glass seem to assemble themselves out of thin air.

Hutchison's torch, or blowlamp, is adjustable to supply an oxygen or a gas flame. The gas flame is used to preheat and soften colored glass rods not much thicker than a pencil lead. The hotter oxygen flame melts the glass more quickly while it is being manipulated, at the same time cleaning off the carbon smudge left by the gas flame. Hutchison holds one end of a thin, green glass rod in the flame until it is heated just enough to be worked. Then, deftly, gently he pulls out the hot tip of the thin rod with tweezers, extending about an inch of the end, which remains attached to the rod by a fine hair of glass. Then he pinches the green extension with flat, brass flattening tongs—and lo and behold a green leaf! Now the green glass rod is really an opaque white rod with a translucent green coating, so that at the tip of Hutchison's leaf the interior white shows, and this is not desirable. White leaf tips were a frequent flaw in nineteenth century French and American flower paperweights; but Hutchison eliminates them simply by reheating the tip, which seals the green over the white.

Once he has made a selection of separate design parts—leaves, flower petals, stems, insect wings—Hutchison can assemble his flowers and insects by fusing the parts together according to the predetermined designs. Hutchison has learned which elements to assemble and which to leave separate. He knows that unless a white flower petal is attached in a certain way the petal may shrivel up. But a butterfly is not pre-assembled because, if all the parts were not exactly on a common level, the butterfly might break when covered by the first gather of hot glass. The even more delicate dragonfly, on the other hand, too fragile to bury in hot glass, is instead pre-assembled and placed on the top of a glass ball, which holds it fixed for the next gather.

I watched John Deacons arrange the separate wings, body, and the pre-bent antenna of a butterfly on a flat iron die, which he then covered with a metal cylinder topped by a flat metal sheet, placing it over a gas burner to heat up in preparation for the descent of the pontil rod. Paperweight collectors have noticed how often one of the separately made antennae on a Baccarat butterfly of the 1840s appears detached from the insect. Deacons has the secret for keeping Hutchison's U-shaped antennae attached to the butterfly: he simply lances the hot covering glass with a long needle and forces the antennae to the nose of the insect, then marvers out the hole left by the needle, which would otherwise create a bubble when covered with more glass.

On another occasion Peter McDougall was putting lampworked dahlias in paperweights. The large, pink dahlia appears convincingly three-dimensional, with its three tiers of petals one above another and all above a layer of leaves. To achieve the effect Hutchison has fused together a circle of leaves and three separate circles of petals. The leaves and each of the three petal assemblies was placed in a separate mold, and Peter McDougall picked them up on the pontil in series, each tier gather separated by a marble-sized clear gob of glass attached by the servitor, thus imparting the three-dimensional effect. A downward curve at the center of the flower to a simulated stem can be simply achieved by lancing a needle or pick through the center of the tiered assembly, a simple and effective trick employed by paperweight makers at the turn of the century and by craftsmen in mainland China today.

The final step in decorating some of the more elaborate weights is the cutting done by factory manager Moravec and the young men under him. Tony was born in a likely place for a glassman, Teblic in Czechoslovakia. His grandfather and father had been in the glass business, and on his vacations as a boy of seven or eight Tony had to stack medicine bottles in a lehr (annealing oven). Like many another Czech of the same tender age, Moravec left the old country for Britain, and he has been there ever since.

At fourteen Tony Moravec started in the glass business as an apprentice to a 'brilliant' glasscutter. When he reached twenty-one he was supposed to return to technical college in Czechoslovakia, but, as he says, 'When you're twenty-one you know it all, and I quit.' Instead, Moravec engraved a polar bear on a flat plate of glass; but he achieved it with a 'brilliant' cutting machine, which is generally used for the deep geometrical cutting of punch bowls. He also used the cutting machine on a goldfish bowl he cut as a special order for a magician whose act called for the goldfish to disappear when he tossed them back into the bowl. The disappearance was accomplished by the bowl's having an open space at the bottom that was completely camouflaged by the refractions of Moravec's deep 'brilliant' cutting.

Moravec worked for many years in Leeds, but he really wanted to live in Scotland, and in 1965 he came to work for Stuart Drysdale, who was then managing Strathearn. Moravec began by squashing the Teachers Whisky bottles, but soon was facetting paperweights to show what he could do. Today, in addition to shouldering responsibility for the day to day working of the factory, Tony Moravec supervises the cutting room. His assistants here are Archie Anderson, who has been at Perthshire for five years, and Barry McDougall, formerly with John Moncrieff in Perth and at Perthshire since April, 1973. It was Barry's brother Peter I watched make the dahlia.

Like the other technical aspects of paperweight making, cutting and polishing is a long established process involving a set series of steps.

To facet a single paperweight with punties (flat or concave round cuts) and a starcut base may take from two to four hours, and has to be done with a steady hand and a sharp eye. On plates, bowls, or other thin, transparent vessels cutting is done above the grinding wheel, because the cutter can see through the glass and gauge the effect of what he is doing on both surfaces at the same time. But with a paperweight the distortions of thick glass, and a ground or design that frequently masks the view, requires that the cutting be done below the wheel where the cutter can't see what he's doing. This, appropriately, is called 'blind cutting.' In blind cutting the cutter has often to gauge his work—say the straight but intersecting lines of a cut star—with his fingers held on either side of the aloxite cutting wheel. I watched Moravec cut an almost perfect star in this way, working 'blind,' almost as if he had a built-in gyroscope.

To cut punties on a paperweight four grades of grinding wheel are used. The top punty on a weight has to be cut first to see if the interior design is good enough to justify cutting the rest of the facets. This is especially the case with an overlay, because until a window is cut the design is completely hidden by the overlay. Rough cutting of the facets is done on a diamond-studded lap (lapidary wheel), which grinding obscures the view of the interior and leaves the facet or punty looking like a blizzard seen through a window. Next, rough polishing is done on a small smooth stone kept moist with a water-saturated sponge. Then a big wheel of laminated felt is used, with pumice powder as the polishing agent. Final polishing is done on another felt wheel, using cerium oxide, which is also used to polish optical lenses and is better than the usual rouge powder. Paperweight bases are ground and polished on four graded, flat wheels: an iron disk, a stone wheel lubricated with water, a wooden wheel used with pumice, and finally a flat felt wheel used with cerium oxide. Each grinder (cutter) develops his own pet improvements—one device I noticed was a wet, blue foam rubber kitchen sponge in a little tin box beneath the wheel to keep the wheel moist.

Top left—Ladling glass from furnace
Below—Destroying rejects

In the cutting of punties through a double overlay it is particularly important that the two overlay colors be of uniform thickness over the surface of the weight, to ensure that the interior design is framed in even borders of opaque white inside the color overlay. Drysdale and Moravec were disturbed by several lavender double overlay weights where the outer casing of clear glass that always must cover the outer overlay was too thick and looked clumsy, at the same time diluting the strength of the lavender overlay, as though it had been watered down. Though the interior close millefiori designs of these particular weights were flawless, and all punties were fully ground and polished, the weights were tossed in the reject carton. Aside from the tedious making of the canes, which may have taken weeks, the loss of these 'imperfect' paperweights represented several hours work by several craftsmen.

Friday is the big day at Perthshire, the day they throw the rejects on the dump and empty the furnace tanks in preparation for the next week's melt. But that demonic performance takes place in the afternoon, so on Friday morning I moved about the factory, asking more questions and watching the repetition of ancient tasks of which I find it impossible to tire.

I watched muscular John Irvine and his servitor make a small pitcher with a concentric millefiori design in the bottom. Irvine had worked at Edinburgh Crystal, which he had left in the peripatetic way so common to glassblowers, to give the 'States' a try at Pairpoint, a glassworks on Cape Cod. But Irvine had found the New England summers too hot and returned to Perthshire. Up to that time he had never made a paperweight, but now he does it with ease and the rippling muscles of his bare arms. I watched Irvine blow the pitcher, sheer off the top, heat the uneven edge at the glory hole until it became a perfect pitcher lip, with exactly the same curve and flair as countless others he has made. Then, just in time, the servitor appeared from nowhere with a little gob of glass for the pitcher handle, which together they attached and Irvine shaped. A moment later the servitor carried the pitcher to the annealing kiln by its newly made handle, an act that says something about economy of function.

When he finished the pitcher Irvine automatically made a chalk mark on the arm of his glassmaker's chair. I had noticed all the men did this and wondered whether it was a sign of competition. Irvine assured me it was simply a way of keeping track of how many weights he had made that day. But, asking Roy MacDonald the same question, I was not so sure.

Roy MacDonald was one of the original apprentices at Perthshire, along with Peter MacDougall and John Deacons. MacDonald is a rather temperamental perfectionist. Outwardly, sitting in his chair, rolling his pontil forward and backward, shaping the hot glass, he appears as casually skilful as the others. But there is an intensity to his work and he fusses about the paper pad he uses to shape the weights. MacDonald's pad is nothing but a wet wad of tissue paper that has burned out to a shape that fits the curvature of a paperweight's dome, and enables him to shape glass with the finger sensitivity of a sculptor. To the casual eye his pad looks useless, but to MacDonald it almost has the touch of life. He's had his pad for six months now, occasionally feeding it from the back with new paper. The pad has reached the point where it's so charred on the contact surface that a tiny flake of ash is transferred to the surface of the paperweight, and MacDonald removes it with a flick of his wrist that, without his hand touching the glowing surface, creates enough air to lift the ash away. He rolls and shapes his paperweight with caressing tenderness, brooding that soon he'll have to make a new pad.

MacDonald's sense of competition is apparent in the chalk marks he makes on the arm of his chair—there are already today several groups of four vertical strokes with the slash through each group to make five. But it isn't just today's total he's concerned with, MacDonald seems to remember just about every weight he ever made. 'In 1972 I made eleven thousand, two hundred and seventy-four paperweights, including rejects,' he says, adding, 'And that was a bad year.'

Rejects are rejected on Fridays. First, quantities of broken clear and colored glass swept from the blowing room floor are carried outdoors and tossed onto the open dump of broken and coagulated glass, sounding like all the loose change in the world. Then come the cartons of thirty or more rejected weights that Miss Robertson has already knocked together until they are covered with moon bruises. And now they are tossed onto the awful mass. 'You get used to throwing them out,' says Tony Moravec, 'but it grieves me that there are defects in there.'

Meanwhile, back in the blowing room the tanks are being emptied of whatever old glass remains after the week's work. Chick Young, who came to Perthshire in 1973 via Wick and Strathearn, and John Irvine are at the two tanks, each using a long-handled ladle to decant the molten glass, which they ladle into shovels held by the servitors. The incandescent glass glows opalescent as it pours from the ladles into the shovels. This particular Friday the servitors are Alan Laing, a big boy with long hair who happens to be the milkman's son, Scott Anderson, who favours a bright orange shirt, and Harry Mackay, diminutive Stevenson Mackay's only slightly taller older brother. Shod only in holey shoes or old sneakers, they race to the dump with full shovels, hot glass splashing and trailing from the shovels onto the glasshouse floor. Soon the floor is littered with spills of cooling glass that crackles and pops as it passes rapidly below the annealing temperature. Spiders' webs of glass trail from the boys' shoes and shovels.

Each shovelful of hot glass is emptied onto the dump over the paperweights, which explode in loud reports under the viscous blanket, showing through the awful mass like the gelatinous eyes of dead and rotting fish. In the blowing room the spilled glass criss-crosses the floor in ribbons like quicksilver. Watching the tanks being emptied is like watching a living thing die. At Perthshire they throw out thousands of pounds worth of glass every year.

When the tanks are empty the temperature inside rises from about 1240 degrees centigrade to 1340 or 1360 degrees. Whoever is chosen by rotation for weekend duty must now charge the tanks with the sand and chemical ingredients for the new batch of glass, a procedure that takes several hours. The temperature in the tanks continues to rise until it reaches the melting height of 1480 degrees centigrade, which is an infernal 2696 degrees Fahrenheit. At about 6 p.m. on Saturday the new batch is ready for 'boiling.'

Boiling means stirring to get rid of any cords or other irregularities in the batch, and this is done with a long iron bar tipped with a short log of silver birch. To boil the melt the log is first soaked in a bucket of water to retard its consumption in the furnace. Then the log-tipped iron bar is shoved into the furnace and dunked in the molten glass. Instantly a tremendous domed bubble rises to the surface and flashes open with a roar, overturning and clearing the glass, and sending long blasts of flame out from the furnace hole. After about six boilings a birch log is reduced to about a quarter of its original size, and a new log is impaled on the iron bar. I asked if a blast of compressed air directed into the melt would not achieve the same result, and was assured that it would; but old traditions in glassmaking die hard.

With amusement Drysdale told me about the night the man charging the new batch put in some cobalt, which he mistook for the decolorizer manganese. 'We don't use one hundred grains of cobalt in a year. The glass was deep deep blue and it took us four new melts to get it all out. If we'd known beforehand we could have made Bristol bowls that week.'

CHAPTER III

In addition to its common concentrics and scrambleds Perthshire today makes a wide variety of millefiori and lampworked paperweights and related items such as the jugs already described, doorknobs, and scent bottles. There are six varieties of signed and slightly more expensive patterned millefiori paperweights, and some other patterned weights which are dated and made in limited quantities each year. Finally, there are four or five paperweights a year made as 'Restricted Issues' of three hundred to four hundred; and these are never repeated. If less than three hundred examples of an issue are made some collectors are unable to obtain them and inevitably feel left out. Nor would special orders under three hundred be worth the trouble and expense, since it requires twenty or thirty trials before a new weight can be considered good enough for release.

I observed to Stuart Drysdale that with each new 'Restricted Issue' paperweight he was working toward perfection, and that when he achieved it the issue was finished. He agreed. But then I asked him if it didn't become boring to the men to keep repeating the same kinds of paperweight? To which his instant reply was, 'Oh, the employees are fed up with this year's weights already.' I said I considered that a sign of *esprit de corps.*

Perthshire Paperweights is run on a profit-sharing basis, which boosts wages higher than they would ordinarily be in a glass factory. Drysdale fondly recalls that 'When they got their profit-sharing bonus in July, Harry Mackay and his little brother Steve got together and bought their mother a refrigerator.'

Factory costs break down to roughly sixty per cent for wages, thirty per cent for fuel, and ten per cent for materials and supplies. This ratio is perhaps a reversal of the paperweight making situation in the Classic period of the 1840s when wages were often low, fuel was cheap and fuel sources nearby often there for the taking—but the cost of the metal (glass) itself, especially during the days of the heavy glass excise duty, was dear indeed. Even as late as 1960, in his Vasart days, Drysdale was told that to be economically sound, glass in the solid state (that is cooled) had to bring the factory at least two shillings a pound before any other production costs were added. He guesses that perhaps one reason the French and American crown paperweights were hollow blown was to save on glass. Perthshire crown weights are solid because the glass is relatively cheap to make, and also because, technically, there is not much difference between blowing a bubble from an arrangement in a mold, and leaving the gather solid.

Perthshire glass has a low lead content of twelve per cent. But, held to the light, the glass is clear and sparkling, and free of the striae and the corrosive-action inclusions generally associated with high lead content glass, poorly constructed furnaces, and loosely supervised or unbalanced melts. The long range goal is for Perthshire to produce all its own colored glass. At present it brews its own clear glass every week—one tank has been running continuously for two years—and its high grade, arsenic opaque white glass. High quality white is essential for the brilliance of canes and lampworked parts where the opaque white is covered with a layer of translucent color. Drysdale thinks the brilliance of the old canes from the Clichy factory is attributable to the wonderful white that underlaid the colors.

The two grades of white, one for the cheaper, the other for the more expensive weights are melted in two small pots that stand at one end of the blowing room. A shipment of new pots from Stourbridge stands at the other end. I mentioned to Drysdale that every one of the new pots I examined seemed to be cracked. 'You're quite right,' he said, 'We've ordered another lot, but Heaven knows when they'll get here. The peril of a small operation like ours is you're dependent on too many outside people. That's why we want to make all our own color, and eventually our own everything.' And that takes money, time, patience, and perhaps most of all, enthusiasm.

The enthusiasm is there, I hear it in Stevenson Mackay's whistling. I observe Tony Moravec's remarkable patience. And I see that with time the boys in the blowing room are growing into men. As for the money, well, it's only money.

PERTHSHIRE SPECIAL EDITIONS 1969-1975

Page 30

1. Faceted Flower Weight 1973. Issue 600.
2. Dragonfly Weight 1970. Issue 500.
3. Ribbon Weight 1971. Issue 150.
4. Faceted Cushion Ground Weight 1972. Issue 300.
5. Flower and Bud Weight on Lilac Base 1974. Issue 350.
6. Scattered Weight 1974. Issue 500.

Page 31

1. Christmas Mistletoe Weight 1972. Issue 300.
2. Christmas Holly Weight 1971. Issue 250.
3. Flower on Basket Weight 1973. Issue 300.
4. Faceted Carpet Ground Weight 1973. Issue 350.
5. Garland Weight 1974. Issue 350.
6. Close Millifiori Weight 1973. Issue 400.

Page 32

1. Amethyst Double Overlay Close Millifiori Weight 1974. Issue 300.
2. Translucent Overlay Weight 1970. Issue 150.
3. Faceted Dahlia Weight 1972. Issue 200.
4. Overlaid Penguin on Ice Weight 1975.
5. Faceted Weight with Dragonfly on Bouquet 1974. Issue 300.
6. Swan in the Pond Weight 1973. Issue 250.

Page 33

1. Patterned Cushion Ground Weight 1975.
2. Faceted Pansy Weight 1971. Issue 350.
3. Red, White and Blue Crown Weight 1969. Issue 350.
4. Christmas Robin Weight 1974. Issue 325.
5. Dog Rose Weight 1975.
6. Butterfly Weight 1975.

NOT ILLUSTRATED

1. Patterned Cushion Ground Weight 1971. Issue 250.
2. Translucent Amethyst Overlay Bottle 1971. Issue 300.
3. Miniature Flower in Basket Weight 1972. Issue 1,000.

 Perthshire Special editions

Perthshire Special editions

Perthshire Special editions

Perthshire Special editions